How to Be a VIKING

by Nel Yomtov

PEBBLE
a capstone imprint

Pebble is published by Capstone,
1710 Roe Crest Drive, North Mankato, Minnesota 56003
capstonepub.com

Copyright © 2026 by Capstone. All rights reserved. No part of this publication may be reproduced in whole or in part, or stored in a retrieval system, or transmitted in any form or by any means, electronic, mechanical, photocopying, recording, or otherwise, without written permission of the publisher.

Library of Congress Cataloging-in-Publication Data is available on the Library of Congress website.

ISBN: 9798875226823 (hardcover)
ISBN: 9798875234507 (paperback)
ISBN: 9798875234514 (ebook PDF)

Summary: Journey back in time to Scandinavia and become a Viking! Learn about the armor, weapons, and lifestyle of these legendary explorers and find out if you have what it takes to set sail as one of history's fiercest fighters.

Editorial Credits
Editor: Alison Deering; Designer: Bobbie Nuytten; Media Researcher: Svetlana Zhurkin; Production Specialist: Whitney Schaefer

Image Credits
Alamy: Ivy Close Images, 27, North Wind Picture Archives, 28; Getty Images: Alan Morris, 21, Belgium, 20, clu, 4, FXQuadro, 19, gremlin, cover (top), Lorado, 8, 11, 13, 22, ManuelVelasco, 14, meatbull, 9, ratpack223, 7, RockingStock, 24, Viktor Kostenko, 15 (symbol); Shutterstock: adolf martinez soler (stone wall), cover and throughout, Alex_Maryna, 10, 17, Burak Erdal, cover (viking), Eldi D, 15 (sword), Konstantin G, 16, Malcolm Fairman, 23, Viktor Osipenko, 18, Yip Po Yu (texture), cover and throughout

Any additional websites and resources referenced in this book are not maintained, authorized, or sponsored by Capstone. All product and company names are trademarks™ or registered® trademarks of their respective holders.

Table of Contents

Introduction
Welcome to the Viking World............4

Chapter 1
Preparing for Battle..........................6

Chapter 2
Weapons of War............................. 14

Chapter 3
The Viking Life 20

Chapter 4
A Call to Arms! 24

Test Your Viking Knowledge 30
Glossary... 31
Index 32
About the Author 32

Words in **bold** are in the glossary.

Introduction

Welcome to the Viking World

From the late 700s to 1100, Viking warriors **terrorized** northern Europe. They attacked and looted towns. Their victims gave them the name "Vikings." It comes from the Norse word *vikingr*, meaning meaning "pirate" or "raider."

The Vikings came from **Scandinavia**. The area includes the countries of Denmark, Sweden, and Norway.

Vikings were driven by a desire for riches. But they were not just raiders. They were also farmers, sailors, and expert shipbuilders. Their ships could cross huge oceans or sail inland up narrow rivers. No town was safe.

Not all Scandinavians had what it took to become Viking warriors. Do YOU dare apply for the job?

Chapter 1

Preparing for Battle

You live in a small village near the coast of Denmark. Each day you plow fields, lift stones, harvest crops, and care for livestock.

The farming lifestyle prepares you for the challenges of the Viking life. Long walks over the countryside improve your **endurance**. Rowing boats on the sea and rivers hardens your muscles. Your body learns to thrive in harsh winter weather.

Your daily life is filled with activities that improve your speed, strength, and **agility**. Horse riding and **archery** prepare you for the battlefield.

The games and sports you play are also a part of your training. Swimming and tug-of-war build muscle strength. Skiing and ice-skating improve your balance and help build your leg muscles.

You train several times a week using swords, axes, and spears. These practice tools are heavier than the weapons you will use on a **raid**. Training with these will build strength and quickness.

Some days you practice one-on-one **combat** with another warrior from your village. Wrestling matches help you prepare for hand-to-hand combat on the battlefield.

Other times, you train as part of a team. You practice using weapons against neighbors in pretend battles.

You also practice strategies. The shield wall is one important **tactic**. You and your fellow Vikings stand shoulder to shoulder with your shields overlapping. The shields form a wall. It provides both defense and offense. Protected by your shields, the group moves slowly forward to overrun the enemy.

Your leaders judge your training performance. They make you practice your skills until they are perfect and ready for deadly combat.

Tip #1: Be a Berserker!

Berserkers—a special type of Viking—howled, foamed at the mouth, and bit their own shields as they fought. In this frightening state of rage and fury, these wild-eyed Viking warriors nearly scared their enemies to death!

Chapter 2

Weapons of War

Your main weapon is your sword. It is roughly 3 feet (0.9 meters) long. But it only weighs about 3 pounds (1.4 kilograms). It's light enough for you to carry in one hand. You hold a wooden shield in your other hand.

The point of your sword is more **blunt** than sharp. For this reason, the sword is used mainly for cutting rather than stabbing. It is decorated with patterns and letters, such as the letter for the Norse god of war.

The symbol for the Norse god of war

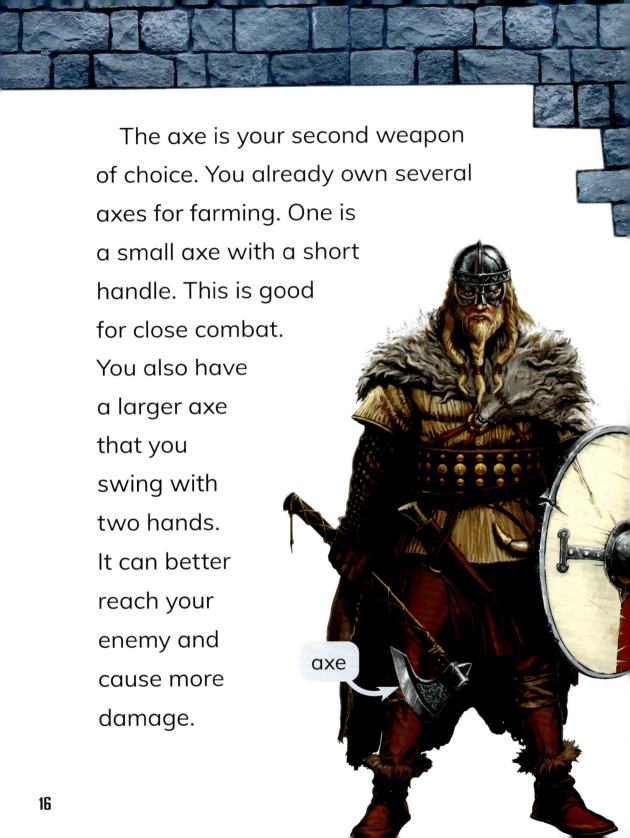

The axe is your second weapon of choice. You already own several axes for farming. One is a small axe with a short handle. This is good for close combat. You also have a larger axe that you swing with two hands. It can better reach your enemy and cause more damage.

axe

Spears are your third most-used weapon. You own a throwing spear and a thrusting spear. The thrusting spear is used in hand-to-hand fighting.

You are a wealthy warrior. This means you can afford a coat of **mail** and an iron helmet. Mail is armor made from many small iron rings. Your helmet is a simple cone shape with nose and eye guards.

You take your mail with you on the raiding ship. But it is hot and heavy to wear while fighting. For this reason, you may decide to leave it on board when the actual battle begins.

Tip #2: What's In a Name?

For good luck in battle, Vikings named their swords. Tales tell of swords named Dragon Slayer, Leg Biter, and many others. What name will you give your trusted sword?

Chapter 3

The Viking Life

When not on a raid, you spend time in your small village. There you farm, fish, and raise animals such as pigs, sheep, and cattle. In a small garden, you and your family grow fruits and vegetables.

You've built a large house called a **longhouse**. Its thick walls are made of wood and mud. They help protect against cold winters. The roof is made with layers of grass, branches, and leaves.

The clothing you wear is simple but sturdy. Your shoes and boots are made from the skins of seals or reindeer. You have tight-fitting pants made of linen or wool. The **tunic** you wear on top is pulled tight at the waist by a leather belt.

Common people in your village wear hats made of felt or wool. As a show of wealth, you often wear a fur-trimmed hat.

Tip #3: Sharpen Your Strategy Skills

Play the chess-like board game called Hnefatafl (NEF-ah-tah-fel) in your spare time. You'll have to take your opponent by surprise to win the game—just as you would on the battlefield!

Chapter 4

A Call to Arms!

The year is 1016. Your Viking leaders order a raid on Essex. It is a wealthy kingdom on the east coast of England. Large amounts of gold objects, jewels, and weapons are yours for the taking.

You and hundreds of fellow Viking warriors set sail. But this attack will not be a surprise. English spies have warned the Essex king that Vikings are coming. Your enemy is eager to push you back into the sea.

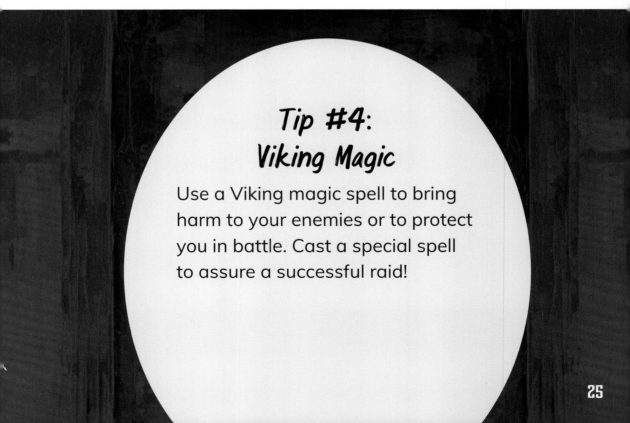

Tip #4: Viking Magic

Use a Viking magic spell to bring harm to your enemies or to protect you in battle. Cast a special spell to assure a successful raid!

Your ships pull up close to the shore. You leap overboard and rush to meet the enemy. But English forces are ready. They unleash a storm of stones, arrows, and spears. Your leaders order you to move forward as a shield wall. Your group rushes forward and breaks through the English line!

It's time for hand-to-hand combat. You attack an enemy soldier with your spear. You hook his shield, rip it from his hand, and toss it aside. You draw your sword. Your enemy draws his.

You're locked in a fight to the finish. The clanging of swords, whizzing of arrows, and shouting of men in battle nearly overpower you. Will you survive today's deadly combat?

Vikings are best remembered as great warriors. But they were also expert sailors and explorers. They set up trade routes across Europe and Asia. They also established major cities, including Dublin, Ireland. Viking explorers even reached North America 500 years before Christopher Columbus.

The Viking tradition was difficult and violent, but it often led to wealth and adventure. Think carefully before you set sail!

Test Your Viking Knowledge

1. What is a berserker?
   a. a Scandinavian fisherman
   b. a type of Viking axe
   c. a Viking warrior who fought in a furious rage

2. What is your main weapon?
   a. a spear
   b. a sword
   c. a bow and arrow

3. What is Hnefatafl?
   a. a board game played to improve strategy skills
   b. a dish made with meat and potatoes
   c. a Viking defensive tactic

4. The three countries of Scandinavia are:
   a. Denmark, England, and Iceland
   b. Denmark, Norway, and Sweden
   c. Denmark, England, and Sweden

5. What is a shield wall?
   a. a stone wall to protect a village
   b. a Viking battle formation
   c. a place to hang a shield when not being used

Answers: 1) c, 2) b, 3) a, 4) b, 5) b

If you answered all the questions correctly, the job of Viking warrior is yours! If not, take another read through this book and try the test again!

Glossary

agility (uh-GI-luh-tee)—the ability to move quickly and easily

archery (AR-chuh-ree)—the practice or skill of shooting with a bow and arrow

blunt (BLUHNT)—having a dull edge or point

combat (KOM-bat)—fighting between people or armies

endurance (en-DUR-enss)—the ability to keep doing an activity for a long period of time

longhouse (LAWNG-hous)—a long, narrow, single-room building

mail (MAYL)—a type of armor made of small metal rings joined together to form a mesh

raid (RAYD)—a sudden, surprise attack on a place

Scandinavia (skan-duh-NAY-vee-uh)—the part of northern Europe that includes Denmark, Norway, and Sweden

tactic (TAK-tik)—a plan for fighting a battle

terrorize (TER-uh-rize)—to frighten someone a great deal

tunic (TOO-nik)—a loose shirt with or without sleeves

Index

armor, 18
axes, 10, 16

Berserkers, 13

clothing, 22

farming, 5, 6, 16, 20
fighting, 11, 12, 16–17, 18, 25, 26, 28

games, 9, 23

lifestyle, 6, 8–9, 20
lodging, 21

naming, 4, 19

raiding, 10, 18, 20, 24

sailing, 5, 6, 25, 29
Scandinavia, 5, 6
shields, 12, 13, 14, 26
spears, 10, 17, 26
strategies, 12, 26
swords, 10, 14–15, 19, 26, 28

training, 9, 10, 11, 12

About the Author

Nel Yomtov is an award-winning author of children's nonfiction books and graphic novels. He specializes in writing about history, current events, biography, architecture, and military history. He has written numerous graphic novels for Capstone, including the recent *The Wright Brothers Take Flight*, *The Christmas Truce of World War I*, and *D-Day Training Turned Deadly: The Exercise Tiger Disaster*. In 2020 he self-published *Baseball 100*, an illustrated book featuring the 100 greatest players in baseball history. Nel lives in the New York City area.